D1170842

WHITE

By Patricia M. Stockland
Illustrated by Julia Woolf

Content Consultant
Susan Kesselring, MA
Literacy Educator and Preschool Director

magic
wagon

visit us at www.abdopublishing.com

Published by Magic Wagon, a division of the ABDO Publishing Group, 8000 West 78th Street, Edina, Minnesota 55439. Copyright © 2009 by Abdo Consulting Group, Inc. International copyrights reserved in all countries. All rights reserved. No part of this book may be reproduced in any form without written permission from the publisher.

Looking Glass Library™ is a trademark and logo of Magic Wagon.

Printed in the United States.

Text by Patricia M. Stockland
Illustrations by Julia Woolf
Edited by Jill Sherman
Interior layout and design by Nicole Brecke
Cover Design by Nicole Brecke

Library of Congress Cataloging-in-Publication Data

Stockland, Patricia M.
  White / by Patricia M. Stockland ; illustrated by Julia Woolf.
     p. cm. — (Colors)
  ISBN 978-1-60270-259-2
  1. White—Juvenile literature. 2. Color—Juvenile literature. I. Woolf, Julia, ill. II. Title.
  QC495.5.S775 2009
  535.6—dc22
                          2008001632

We see the clouds part.

The clouds are white.

4

We put on warm mittens.

Our mittens are white.

We walk through the deep snow.

The snow is white.

8

Our stepdad ties our skates.

Our laces are white.

We race across the pond ice.

The pond ice is white.

12

A rabbit watches us skate.

The rabbit is white.

We wrap up in warm blankets.

The blankets are white.

15

Our stepdad makes hot chocolate with milk.

The milk is white.

We add lots of marshmallows.

The marshmallows are white.

19

We rest on pillows by the fire.

The pillows are white.

What Is White?

There are three primary colors: red, blue, and yellow. These colors combine to create other colors. You cannot mix other colors to make pure white. You can mix white with other colors to make them lighter.

Primary Colors

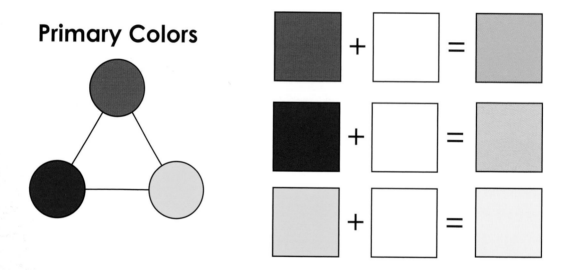

What white things did you see in the story?

Words to Know

blanket—a soft, warm covering.

hot chocolate—a warm, sweet drink.

pillow—a soft pad.

skate—a boot with a blade on the bottom for gliding on ice.

Web Sites

To learn more about the color white, visit ABDO Publishing Company on the World Wide Web at **www.abdopublishing.com**. Web sites about the colors are featured on our Book Links page. These links are routinely monitored and updated to provide the most current information available.